T0128643

CARTOON CAPERS to COLOR

To order additional copies of this book, contact:
Xlibris
844-714-8691
www.Xlibris.com
Orders@Xlibris.com

ISBN: Softcover 978-1-4134-8708-4

Print information available on the last page

Rev. date: 08/17/2022

CARTOON CAPERS TO COLOR

is the property of
Marvin A. Berg Sr. and P.C. Berg

Printed in the United States of America

Verses
by
P.C. Berg

This Silly Bird
Really had a surprise
When he tried to use
A pencil this size.
MARVIN BERG
Copyright©
1

When Tommy the Tiger
Steps up to bat
Fans start loud cheering
For the best cat.

MARVIN BERG

Dixie Doggie
Tries a new trick
As a circus performer
He must do his act quick.
Marvin Berg
Copyright ©
3

BEWARE
Buster the Bull
Is warning all
To stay away
Or danger befall.
4
MARVIN BERG
Copyright©

Clinky the Clown
Brings many a smile
With clothes and an act
And a laughable style.
MARVIN BERG
Copyright ©
5

Such a bull may
not be seen,
except perhaps
on Halloween.
6
Copyright

Danny the Donkey
Is as glad as can be,
His numbers just won
the BIG Lottery.

Clarice the Chicken
Dances and sings,
To see her perform
Is really "something".
MARVIN BERG
Copyright ©
8

Bixby the Bowler
Really rolls a fine game,
He has great delivery,
A good arm and sure aim
Marvin Berg
Copyright©
9

Peter the Penquin
Sure needs an oar,
Will this icicle
Help get him to shore?
MARVIN BERG
Copyright©
10

Sailor Fish
Is standing by
Ready to help
If he hears a cry.

11

Barney the Bird
Plays hockey just great,
When he nets a goal
The fans celebrate.
4
MARVIN BERG
Copyright ©
12

Flip and Fin are funny fish,
they like angling too.
They bait their hooks,
but not for friends,
they're out to land a you.

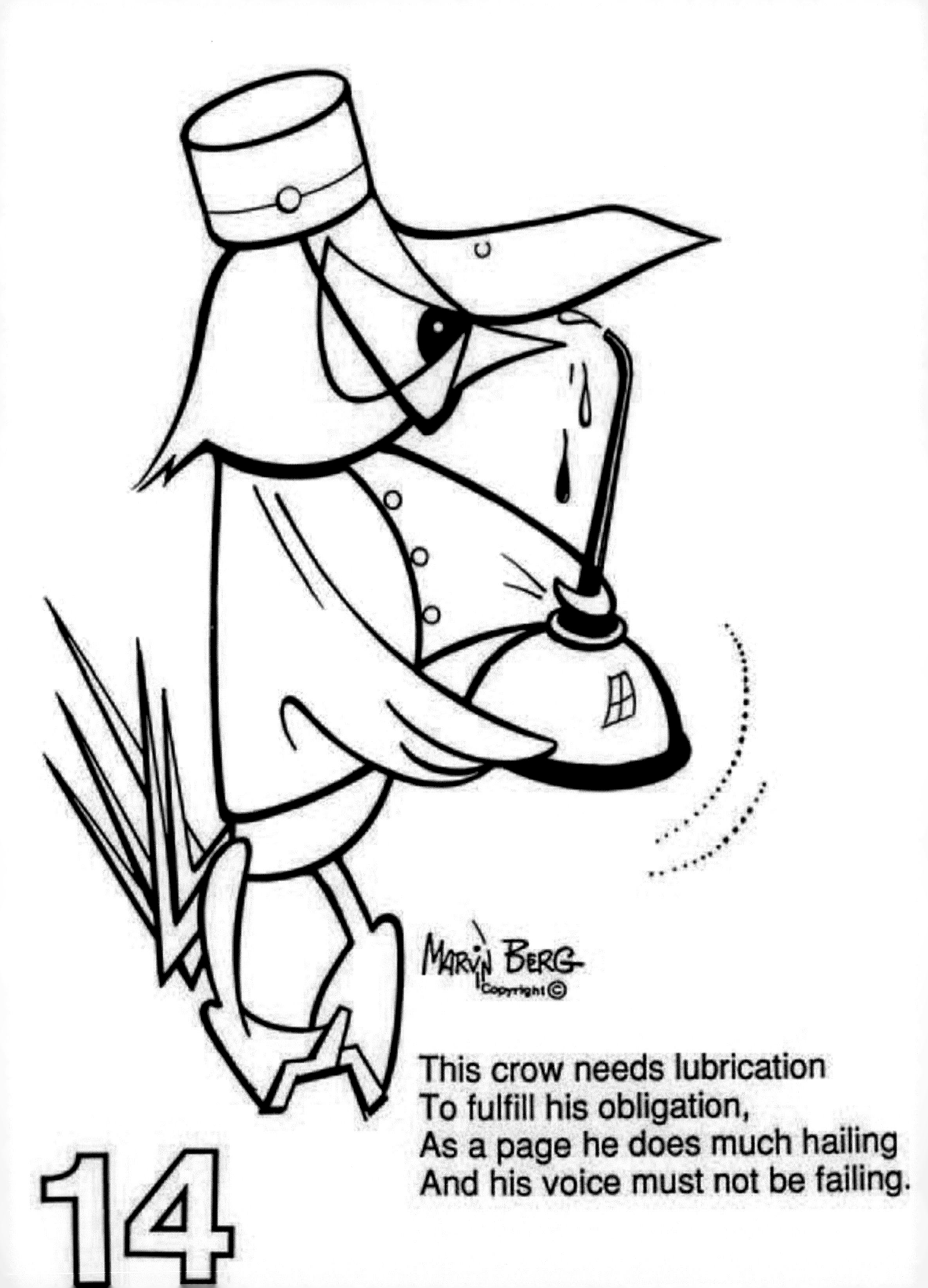
MARVIN BERG
Copyright ©
This crow needs lubrication
To fulfill his obligation,
As a page he does much hailing
And his voice must not be failing.
14

Gary The Golfer
Always has fun
But today's special bonus
His first hole-in-one.
Marvin Berg
15

Gordy the Golfer,
Try as he might,
Has little success
Doing it right.

WATCH FOR
CARTOON CAPERS TO COLOR

Printed in the United States
by Baker & Taylor Publisher Services